Love Letters

& Suicide Notes

Tarra Cornell

BookLeaf Publishing

India | USA | UK

Presentation by *BookLeaf Publishing*

Web: www.bookleafpub.com

E-mail: info@bookleafpub.com

ISBN : 9789358360820

First edition 2022

This book Is dedicated to the survivors, the dreamers, and my family - who made me both.

One

some days my soul longs to go home

while my body is laying in my bed

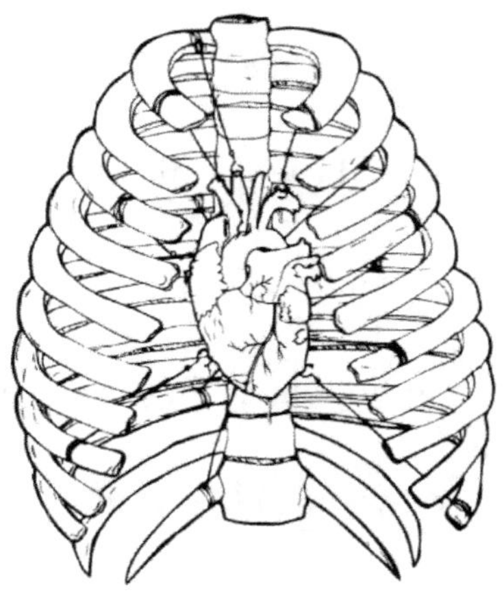

Two

we're just ugly people

trapped in ugly hells

with paperweight poems

holding us together

we wander these midnight gardens

and starlit seas

looking for something beautiful

we want to feel whole

to look in the mirror

and find something beautiful too

to see those gardens in our eyes

and the waves in our skin

self love is not that easy

the mirror is a place of loathing

our minds a twisted labyrinth

we cut ourselves open

drown in liquor and pills

searching for an escape

the world pushes self love on us

as if it were a religion

and we must believe

but believing is not something that comes
easy

sometimes self love is finally showering

after a week of avoiding it

it is going to bed before midnight

cuddling a childhood bear

it is crying your eyes out

it is pulling yourself off the bathroom floor

ignoring the razor

putting the cap on the bottle

self love is not always a hashtag

and embracing all your flaws

sometimes it is quietly ignoring your inner
critic

wearing what you please

saying no

self love is finally believing

you are worthy

oh

we're just beautiful people

trapped in beautiful hells

Three

she has a mouth for a gun

bullet teeth

an amputated heart

beating in a jar of anxiety

she stands tall

using words as weapons

until the lights go low

she says she's not enough

asks if she is too much

crawling into my arms

she weeps

is anyone listening

I say I am

she holds the jar between us

curling around it

my arms around her

are you safe

her voice is a whisper

please be safe

is she talking to me

or the jar

I don't think I'll ever know

Four

I want to write

no

I need to write

my heart roars against the cage

in my chest

I sit on the bathroom floor

staring at the shower that has been dry for

weeks

my stomach aches

I chew on the inside of my mouth

on my lips

until I taste blood

there is no silence

never

my mind whirls

screams at me

write

write

write

I pull words from my wounds

paint them in gold

am I beautiful yet

I write in the middle of a hurricane

on the dance floor

you're mad at me that I can't let the words
be

but if I don't write it now

maybe I'll choke on them

spit them up like clots

maybe I'll forget

the way the wind picked up

just like my pulse

as your body moved with the music

sweat beading on your lip

your back to everyone but me

when our lips meet

I push my words into your mouth

I wonder

will they make you drunk

make your heart ache

make you hang on the strokes of my pen

it feels so good to write

I need this release

this validation

give them something to remember you by

maybe they'll see you

tell me I'm not worthless

tell me

I'm not alone

I can't be lonely

with my words on your lips

dancing around your mind

I need to write

Five

we have remained soft

even with a mouthful of blood

bones breaking beneath

the weight of the world on our shoulders

we smile

and say more

give me all you've got

14

I can carry more

15

Six

I still dream about them

screaming

and all their hands

and lips

when I'm alone I feel like I don't exist

maybe none of it was real

maybe I'm not real at all

maybe I'm not real at all

Seven

if there is a god

if there is anything out there

controlling this

I hope I meet them

bring them to their knees

they will beg my forgiveness

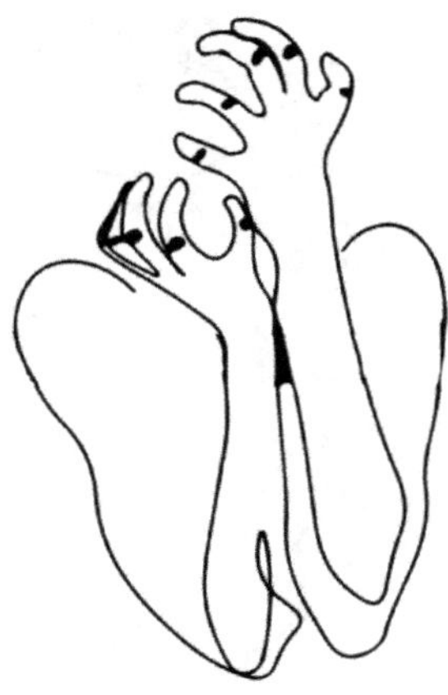

Eight

words can look like poetry

and still taste like poison

Nine

I started planning my funeral

before I even started to bloom

like I was born a ghost

or maybe they made me into one

I can't remember

they told me I was holy

then burnt me to the ground

you don't destroy the things you love

but love isn't grown men

touching children

wrapping big hands around small throats

you can't say you love someone

if you only give them fear

broken bones and shattered glass

I wrote a will in crayon

a grave sounded safer

than my bed

Ten

I am forgetful

I speak in apologies full of prose

when I write I break open

I don't mean to forget

your birthday

or our anniversary

to feed the fish

or shower   (last week)

but I remember

the story of the day your father died

the way the blue sky

made you rage

I remember

the smell of rum on my mother's lips

the feel of summer rain on my skin

and mud between my toes

all my plants are dead   (sorry)

there's a pile of laundry on my floor

and half written poems

scattered around my room

I can't remember

but I won't forget

25

Eleven

I'm full of bad habits

like not thinking before I speak

and not showering for a week (or three)

I fall in love too easily

with everyone that smiles at me

(I planned our wedding the day we met

I still know exactly what dress I'd wear)

I can't sleep when I should

instead I count the scars around my heart

and I'd tell you about them

if I could

but you know some things

are better left unsaid

(at least that's what I say to the demons in
my head)

I spend money on things I don't need

just to feel like I can breathe

(I have to keep breathing)

break open my ribs

pull out all the sadness

(please don't get it on you)

pump my veins full of dopamine

until there's nothing left of me

I'm nothing but bad habits

tarra.cornell@hotmail.comwrapped up in a strangers sheets

Twelve

there's no polite way

to tell your mother that you want to die

while she's screaming over dirty dishes left
in the sink

I wonder if she knows

I was too busy scrubbing blood out of the
shower drain

to put my hands in soapy water

to be honest I forgot they existed

she yells like a banshee

and I scream back

because that's what we do

I want to crawl into her lap and weep

tell her about the people who hurt me

the man who broke into my bedroom

brandishing a gun out of love (so he said)

but never sent a birthday card

the girl at school (I still remember her
name)

and the way she would stab me beneath the
desk

it hurt more than any razor had

the man who held one hand around my
throat

and the other between my thighs

until I thought I would die

the boy who she trusted who didn't
understand "no"

I woke up with bloody thighs

while she made him eggs for breakfast

would she believe me if I showed her

where every hand has burned me

it's right there

a brand that won't ever leave

where every person took what they wanted

and left me for dead

I wonder if she would feel my pulse race

an urgent bug scuttling from the light

a fast pitter-patter just beneath my skin

sometimes I think if I cut deep enough I can
find that bug and pull it out

would she wipe my tears

or pick a fight about my laundry on the
floor

(I'm a mess)

(I'm lazy)

(Why don't I help out more?)

I slam my door and scream and scream

I want to stop and apologise

to tell her I'm not mad at her

that I will do the dishes (later, maybe)

and I will do all the laundry (tomorrow)

because right now I'm drowning

I wonder if I'll write about that in my
suicide note

no

there's no polite way

to tell your mother you want to die

Thirteen

sometimes you feel like a storm

trapped inside skin

you can't quite explain

the lightning in your voice

or the tsunami in your eyes

because no one asks for a hurricane

when they can barely handle a little rain

Fourteen

they want you to be the cool girl

the fun girl

the I don't give a fuck girl

confident girl

coy girl

manic pixie dream girl

don't take your shit girl

satin and lace lingerie girl

leather and whips girl

never been touched before girl

tell me you love me girl

leave me alone girl

smart girl

I need you girl

dominant girl

submissive girl

the artsy girl

the damsel in distress girl

independent girl

sexy girl

your friends want to fuck me girl

marry me girl

the casual fling girl

bend me over the car girl

take me to meet your parents girl

soft girl

hard girl

loud girl

quiet girl

thin girl

thick girl

love me and leave me girl

you'll never forget me girl

Fifteen

he says I'm easy to talk to

his hands on my bare back

as I think of ways to leave

he's already asking about my family

I offer him a smile

an apology

a plea

as I slip into the night

a ghost of the girl I used to be

I scrub my body until I bleed

trying to forget his hands

the way I've forgotten his name

and I wonder how he'd look in a suit

or down on his knees

but he won't call

and I'll wonder why

I don't even remember the colour of his eyes

ocean blue

or moss green

maybe the darkest brown I've ever seen

he asks what I like

I tell him what he wants to hear

hoping that when I ask what he likes

he'll say me

I've already planned our wedding

and my escape route

I tell him he's easy to talk to

my hands in his hair

he says I'm easy to leave

Sixteen

there's a girl

sitting in the bar

hair tied away from her face

she was beautiful

I didn't want to fuck her

I wanted to know her

to buy her a drink

ask about her jeans

she curls in on herself

the sobs shake her

a hurricane of emotion

trapped in a porcelain girl

I'm not good at this

I don't know what to say without crying too

so I touch her arm

because that is comforting

right?

she cries about the world

about women

and I know

we are born from the same festering wound

grown up on the same battlefield

meeting monsters in men

you don't owe anyone forgiveness

you don't need apologies

her smile makes my heart ache

when our eyes meet in the mirror

she looks just like me

and I finally understand

I just want to be seen

Seventeen

my mother told me she looked fat

and I didn't understand

because I thought she looked beautiful

until she gripped pieces of her flesh

and shook them like jelly

her voice full of disgust

she told us it would be healthier

if we cut out carbs and weighed our meals

counted calories and drank weight loss
shakes

(they tasted like powder and sadness)

I was still a child when I learnt

my thighs were too big

tree trunk thighs

thunder thighs

cover them up

I wanted to cut parts of them away

be thinner

more desirable

and my sister had a belly

that seemed normal for a child

but she wore baggy shirts

and spat the word fat like a curse word

I hid chocolate in my underwear drawer

snuck shameful bites in the night

(it's something I still do

I don't know how to stop)

girls like us had to be

funny

smart

generous

(we had enough of ourselves to give and

give and give)

they would say

lucky you have a pretty face

and our parents would yell

why hadn't we eaten our lunches at school

but my sister still can't eat in front of

strangers

and I didn't like hiding in the bathroom

just to eat a sandwich

they say fat like a jinx

like that's all we are

cover it with words like

curvy

voluptuous

thick

to make it desirable

because they can't say fat

without a grimace

as if fat is only bad

my mother still stands before me

asking if she looks fat

pinching at the skin of her stomach

(she grew three babies there)

she spits the word fat and frowns

she looks sad

I think she is beautiful

Eighteen

when you ask me how I am I tell you

I'm fine

and what I mean to say is that

I've taken all my pills

I haven't thought about dying today

and I think our hands fit perfectly together

especially in the dark

when I feel like I'm floating away

that I am planting fields of lavender
between my ribs

because I heard it's good for anxiety

so maybe I can breathe again

without stealing the oxygen from your lips

or taking valium

what I'm trying to say

is that my memories didn't leak into my

dreams

I didn't wake up crying into my pillow

about the monsters I've met in real life

so I got a solid two hours of sleep last night

and I thought about messaging you at 3am

again

my fingers itch

my mind is a merry-go-round

thoughts swirling endlessly

horses going nowhere racing towards you

I've never known how to slow my thoughts

down

without carving them into my skin

or trying to drown in the bath

but my body has always betrayed me

bursting forth

exploding from the water

gasping for air

like I'm being reborn

there my mind goes again

I'm fine

I'm fine

I promise

I'm fine

Nineteen

I. please don't worry about me

II. I showered today and scrubbed my skin
raw until I felt like someone new

III. you know I haven't been well and that I
hate goodbyes

IV. the pets have enough food to last them
months and I have your name carved into
my skin

V. we both know this has been coming for a
long time but it will be okay we will both be
okay

VI. I've been too scared to leave

VII. sometimes I Imagine my future and it's
full of laughter and children and love

VII. sometimes I Imagine my future and
there is nothing but darkness

VIII. sometimes I think of my past and
think of all the things I could've been and

should've been and would've been

IX. I forgive you and I forgive me but I will
never forgive him

X. please don't worry about me

Twenty

I want to write you a love letter

but I don't know where to begin

I guess this is as good a place as any

with an apology

I'm sorry

my heart aches when I think of how I've
treated you

when I think of how others have treated you

I have neglected you

and starved you

you ached with hunger and I ignored you

made you spend days motionless

because moving meant living

and sometimes that is too much

ignoring your needs

not showering or brushing my teeth for
weeks

I blamed you for the pain

accused you of betraying me

I tried to flee from the war beneath my skin

so I made you suffer

when all you have done is hold me together

today I told you I loved you

I let my hands run over your curves and
lumps

touching myself with gentleness and love

there were no razors breaking skin

no uncles or friends claiming you like
unspoilt land

running soft fingers over scars

remnants of the ways we have survived

whispering apologies

a mantra of love

you are worth more than the size of your
jeans

you are worth more than the lovers

left behind like a trail of breadcrumbs

you have not lost value because of the hands
that touched you

you are no less valuable because you didn't
fight or scream

your wounds are real even if you never
fought

even if no one can see them

I want to tell you I'm sorry

I am so sorry

your four year old body did nothing to
deserve this

your eight year old body did nothing to
deserve this

your seventeen year old body did nothing to
deserve this

your twenty-five year old body did nothing
to deserve this

my body did nothing to deserve this

let me tell you this

you do not only exist for others

you are my body

mine

and this self love revolution will not be
loud

it will be you and me

falling in love

quietly

Twenty One

I wonder if anyone will read this

if any one has heard

the promises I have made in the dark

a hundred times

I won't die tonight

because as much as I want to leave

I have nowhere else to go

Twenty Two

I do not know what to do

with the wild thing that sleeps in me

Twenty Three

I want to make art so beautiful

that you mourn when it is no longer

about you

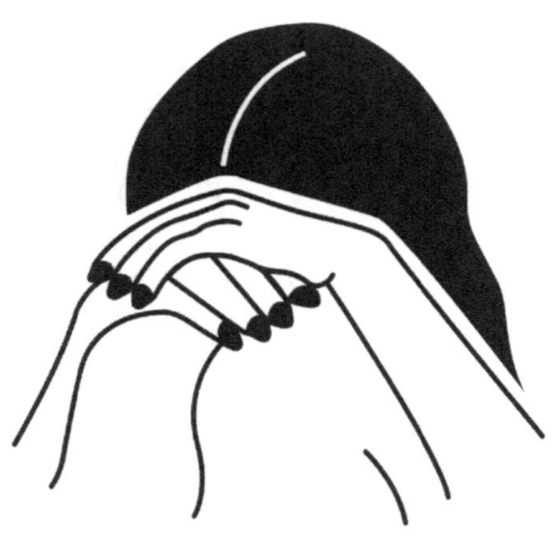

Twenty Four

nothing that happened to me is
beautiful

I try and paint it gold

let me make it easy for you to
understand

if flowers bloomed where pain lived

my body would be a garden

red roses would bloom between my
thighs

where he forced my legs apart

vines wrapping around my wrists

where I tried to cut the hate out of

me

orchids grow along my ribs

blooming where heavy bodies crush

mine

a water lily struggles through the

mud of my heart

beauty can grow through pain

peonies are scattered across my skin

every bruise turned beautiful

and daisies

oh the daisies

break through the cracks in my heart

of my soul

daisies growing everywhere

it's not beautiful the way they tore

me apart

took what they wanted

left me for dead

but I can grow back beautiful

I can water this garden

Twenty Five

I want you naked

I want to see every scar and story on
your skin

I want to see your soul laid bare

I want you at 2am

drunk

clothes scattered across the floor

caution to the wind

that's when you will take me into
your labyrinth

show me your demons

one by one

all the things you're terrified to talk
about

civilised society says you must bury
deep

I want to know your darkness

your sadness

let me meet your sins

and your torments

everything you fear

everything that has ever broken you

I won't make it better

I can't

I want to be there for you at 4pm

I want to listen

and hold you

and tell you that I have demons too

your sadness and your sins don't sit

alone

I want to tell you

your body is a work of art

your soul is crafted by stardust

dinosaur bones

the ocean

things much bigger than you or me

and that makes you infinitely more

beautiful

and important than you think you are

and that no matter when

in the middle of the night or end of
the day

no matter what you say

I will love you

naked